encountering
'the Other'

a time for dying;
a time for planting,
a time for uprooting what has been
planted.
A time for killing;
a time for healing;
a time for knocking down,
a time for building.
A time for tears;
a time for laughter;
a time for mourning,
a time for dancing.
A tim efor throwing stones away,
a time for gathering them up;
a time for embracing,
a time to refrain.

A time for searching
a time for losing;
a time for keeping;
a time for throwing away.
A time for tearing,
a time for sewing;
a time for speaking.
A time for loving,
a time for hating;
a time for war,
a time for peace.

JEAN VANIER

PAULIST PRESS
New York / Mahwah, N.J.

Cover design by Trudi Gershenov
Text design by Niamh McGarry

Copyright © Jean Vanier, 2005

This edition published by arrangement with Veritas
Publications, 7/8 Lower Abbey Street, Dublin I, Ireland,
Email: publications@veritas.ie, Website: www.veritas.ie

The text of this book is adapted from Jean Vanier's talks at
the *Encountering 'the Other'* Conference held in Derry, at the
University of Ulster at Magee, in 2004.

Library of Congress Cataloging-in-Publication Data

Vanier, Jean, 1928-
Encountering 'the other' / Jean Vanier.
p. cm.
ISBN 0-8091-4409-3 (alk. paper)
I. Multiculturalism—Religious aspects—Christianity.
2. Christianity and the other religious.
3. Religious pluralism. I. Title.
BR115.C8V36 2006
261—dc22
2005034087

Published in 2006 by
Paulist Press
997 Macarthur Boulevard
Mahwah, New Jersey 07430

www.paulistpress.com

Printed and bound in the United States of America

Contents

I have waged this war against myself for many
years.
It was terrible, but now I am disarmed.
I am no longer frightened of anything because love
banishes fear.
I am disarmed of the need to be right
And to justify myself by disqualifying others.
I am no longer on the defensive holding onto my
riches.
I just want to welcome and to share.
I don't hold onto my ideas and projects. If
someone shows me something better —
No, I shouldn't say better, but good —
I accept them without any regrets
I no longer seek to compare.
What is good, true and real is always
for me the best.
That is why I have no fear.
When we are disarmed and dispossessed of self,
if we open our hearts to the God man who makes
all things new
then he takes away past hurts
And reveals a new time where everything is
possible.

Patriarch Athenogoras of Constantinople

Introduction

The reflections in this book come from Jean Vanier's talks at a conference held in Derry-Londonderry in June 2004 entitled 'Encountering the Other'. Other keynote speakers were Milorad Todorovic from Kosovo, Aaron Barnea from Israel and Mubarak Awad from Palestine.

This conference enabled people from many religious backgrounds and nationalities to come together and encounter difference and explore and celebrate that difference. The conference revealed that when we encounter we come to know. When we come to know we are able to understand. When we understand, healing and peace can really grow. Peace cannot be imposed by politicians or Churches. Peace has to grow within each person if it is to endure. Our society can only be healed when each person in it is healed. That healing comes not from avoidance or separation, but from encountering.

This book is offered to the reader as a lasting fruit of the conference and as an encouragement and inspiration to encounter the other and so be peacemakers. The style of the book is faithful to Jean's spoken word.

The conference was organised by Anne Gibson, Mary Good, Perpetua McNulty, Ruth Patterson, Simon Coveney and Paul Farren.

CHAPTER I

Daring to Trust
and to Let Go of Power

*To be holy and to be whole. To find one's own
unity inside of oneself, to find unity so that
we're not just in the head or just in the flesh,
not just in the heart; that inner wholeness is a
type of peace and wisdom. And we need
wisdom.*

I joined the royal navy in 1942, when I was thirteen. I crossed the Atlantic at a time when one ship in five was being sunk. Before going I went to my father and I asked him if I could join the navy. He asked 'Why?' I don't remember my answer; what I remember is that he said, 'I trust you. If that is what you want, you must do it. I trust you.' So for me the whole question of peace-making is centred on trust. Trust that you are important, that you are precious, that you have something important to give to the world, to give to me. If we don't believe we are precious, what happens? We have anguish.

For me, the message of the Gospel is that each one of us has a gift to give; each one is precious; each one needs to be loved and to belong.

The fundamental principle of peace is a belief that each person is important. Even if you cannot speak, even if you cannot walk, even if you've been abandoned, you have a gift to give to the other. Do you believe you are important? Do you believe – do we all believe – that we can do something to make this world a better place? Why is the gap between the rich and the poor, the powerful and the powerless growing? There can be no peace unless we can become aware of where this growing gap comes from.

Sometimes those of us who have more power, more money, more time or more knowledge bend down to those who have less power, less knowledge or less wealth; there is a movement from the 'superior' to the 'inferior'. When people are generous they are in control. You can imagine someone in the street falling down and you going to help that person to get up. Then something happens. As you listen to that person you become friends. Perhaps you discover that he or she is living in squalor and has little money. You are not just being generous, you are entering into a relationship, which will change your life. You are no longer in control. You have become vulnerable; you have come to love that person. You have listened to her story. You have been touched by that incredible, beautiful person who has lived something incredibly difficult. You are no longer in control, you are no longer just the generous one, you have become vulnerable. You have become a friend.

There is a very moving text in the Gospel of Luke. Jesus says when you give a meal don't invite the members of your family, your friends or rich neighbours. When you give a really good meal, a banquet, invite the poor, the disabled and the blind and you will be blessed. (Luke 14) In biblical language to give a meal, or to be at a meal, is to become a friend. It is to enter into a covenant relationship. So Jesus is asking us to come up from behind the walls of our group and open our hearts to those who have been marginalised because of their poverty, because of their handicaps, and become their friend. In the heart of Christ there is a yearning to bring people together to meet as friends. To make that move from generosity to communion of hearts will imply a new way of living. It will imply a transformation, because we will have lost power.

CHAPTER 2

Disability and Inequality

By one of those mysteries of life, I was drawn to people with disabilities. Through living with them, sharing with them, laughing with them, struggling with them, praying with them and working with them I have been transformed.

After I left the navy I went to visit a priest who was the chaplain at a small institution for people with mental disabilities. He suggested I come to meet them; I was a little bit anxious because I knew how to drive an aircraft carrier, I knew quite a bit about Aristotle, but I knew very little about people with disabilities! I said to myself, 'Will they be interested? How do you speak with people who do not speak? How will we communicate?' And so I came with anxiety, but when I met them I was very moved because they greeted me warmly and asked me some very fundamental questions: 'Do you love me? Am I important for you?' and then 'Why? Why am I like this? Why can't I live with my Mummy and my Daddy? Why do I fall on the ground? Why?' I felt that it was important during those few days to go into that question of 'Why?' It's an accident of birth – is that a good enough answer?

I have learned so much through living with people with disabilities. I have seen the pain of their hearts. I remember visiting an institution in Brazil; at ten o'clock one morning I entered a small room filled with forty beds and I heard no one crying. I said to myself, 'Forty children, and nobody is crying!' and then I realised that the forty children were in depression. You see, you only cry out if you hope somebody will hear you. If you do not know that somebody will hear you, you will fall into depression. I see so much depression in our modern world.

There is a beautiful story of a young man with a disability who wanted to win the Special Olympics; he got to the hundred metre race and he was running like crazy to get that gold medal. One of the others running with him slipped and fell; he turned round and picked him up and they ran across the finishing line together last. Are we prepared to sacrifice the prize for solidarity? It's a big question. Do we want to win or do we want to be in solidarity with others? Why is the gap between the rich and the poor growing? Or the gap between the powerful and the powerless? Between those who are the oppressors and the oppressed? We have to look at the poorest and the weakest. They have a message to give us. Living with these people — different, fragile, vulnerable, anguished people — has revealed what is the most beautiful in me, but also what is the most terrible. I have discovered that the anguish of some people with disabilities has awoken my anguish.

We need transformation because there is so much tension and egoism in us. We see the world only through our own eyes; we are not liberated to see people as God sees them. We see people through our wounds, through our difficulties, through our prejudices. We need to be liberated to see people with disabilities as God sees them. To see people of other cultures as God sees them. To be liberated in the way we look at them and seek to understand them. We all have fears and prejudices. It is important to discover where our anger and violence came from and how to live with them. It is important to find a way of transformation so that fear and hate can be transformed into positive energies. It's a long road. The water has to be changed into wine. The whole of the vision of Jesus, which is the vision of peace, is about coming out from behind barriers and discovering people as they are. That is the promise that had been foretold through great prophets like Isaiah and Ezekiel: 'I will remove the heart of stone in you and give you a heart of flesh.' I will put my spirit within you. (Ez 36) The spirit of God will be given, so that then we will see people, not through the glasses of our impoverished humanity and our wounds, but as God sees them. It's a transformation. And to enter into the world of transformation we need to want it.

God gave man and woman the incredible gift of bringing children into the world, of loving and educating. Sometimes, however, parents can be disappointed by their children and want them to be other than they are. I have seen the great disappointment in parents when their child is born with a disability. I can understand their pain. However, there is always the danger that parents want to control the lives of their children too much. They forget that to love someone is not to possess or control them, but to help them become more fully themselves and to be proud of who they are.

I heard a story about a boy at a special Communion service in a church in Paris: after the service there was a family gathering with coffee and tea. The boy's uncle went up to his mother and said: 'Wasn't it a beautiful service? The only thing that's sad is that he didn't understand anything.' With tears in his eyes, the little boy said, 'Don't worry Mummy, Jesus loves me as I am.' He knew that he didn't have to be what others wanted him to be, that it was okay to be just himself with his handicaps, his fragility, and all that he was.

I also remember another story of a man who was a successful banker. He had a wonderful marriage and beautiful kids. Everything was going his way, financially, work-wise, family-wise. Then his eldest son began to suffer from a psychotic disorder and was admitted into a psychiatric hospital. The man was furious, because he couldn't control this. He'd always controlled his life. He'd controlled the family, was in control at work, and had been a success. He knew that he had power. But suddenly he realised that he was powerless and a new anguish and anger came out. Then something happened: he met other parents who were living a similar situation and this gradually changed him. Today that man is no longer a successful, powerful banker; that doesn't mean anything to him now. All he wants now is to work with others for a world where there is more love and where his son can be better looked after, where he can find a community.

'Love your enemies, do good to those who hate you, speak well of those who speak evilly of you and pray for those who persecute you' (Luke 6); I have been helped by people with intellectual disabilities; they are a group of people who are not often respected in their deepest needs, not listened to nor held in honour. Paul's first letter to the Corinthians compares the body of the Church with the physical body. He says that those parts of the body which are the least presentable and the weakest are indispensable and should be honoured (cf 1 Cor 2). What an incredible vision! Those who are the weakest are indispensable to the Church and should be honoured. If we walk with those who have been the most crushed, then something will happen within us. I call you to take seriously how beautiful you are, even with all your wounds and weaknesses and the call to honour those who are the weakest.

How to help children become themselves. How to help children develop their inner conscience. We must encourage them to seek the truth, justice and love; to seek mercy and forgiveness so that they become fully themselves, and develop their inner conscience in that place where God lives within them – what I call their 'sacred sanctuary'. We are called to help children. We are called to discover who they are, how beautiful they are and that they are called to open their hearts to love, open their hearts to God. The glory of human beings is not power, the power to control someone else; the glory of human beings is the ability to let what is deepest within us grow. Like that little boy with his friend who came in last in the hundred metre race because he accepted not to win, but wanted solidarity.

CHAPTER 3

Overcoming Our Fear

Our fundamental problem is our consciousness of death. I am not just talking about 'in so many years time I'll be buried'. I'm talking about accepting weakness and growing old, growing into nothingness. Maybe the greatest fear we have is of not being considered worthy, of not being respected. So the fear of death, of being pushed aside, of not being wanted, is very fundamental. We have to look at that whole question of where we are in respect to death.

I believe that what is important today is that we uncover the violence within us and discover that under the violence there is something very beautiful. One of the questions that always comes up is, 'What do we fear?' One of the questions that I like to ask all the people of our communities is, 'What are you most frightened of? Is it fear of not being respected? Is it fear of being put aside? Is it fear of not being loved? Is it fear of death?' What is it that we're frightened of? Because from fear and anguish can rise hate and from hate can rise war.

We must learn how to look into our fears because we cannot let ourselves be controlled by fear. We have to look our fears right in the face and we can't always do it by ourselves. We need to be helped, because if we can't look death and failure in the face, well, then we can never live because to live means to risk, to do things, to have projects which might fail, which might go wrong. We cannot be totally secure for everything; we must discover inside ourselves this power that we have been given to receive the Holy Spirit, not alone, but with others in community, to decide to go forward and to risk things.

The Word became flesh and dwelt amongst us and then we see that the whole of the vision of Jesus is bringing people together. Let me go back to the book of Genesis. It's important to go back to our beginnings: 'in the beginning God made the heavens and the earth'. In the beginning God made man and woman, so that they become one. Then we hear of how man and woman turned away from God because they wanted autonomy rather than to come together in God and with God. They turned away. As they turned away from God, God started calling Adam, 'Where are you?' Adam replied, 'I was frightened because I was naked and I hid.' (Gen 3:9-10) What true words: 'I was frightened.' All of us know the place of fear that is within us. We are frightened. We are frightened of the other, of the one who is different. And why? Because we are so vulnerable. Vulnerable to pain, to failure, to rejection and to death. 'I was naked', Adam was saying 'I was vulnerable. I was in anguish. I didn't know what to do so I hid.' This is the history of humanity. We hide behind walls, behind groups, behind culture. We can even hide behind religion.

But the 'enemy' can become a friend. One of the women who has most influenced me is a young Jewish woman, Etty Hillesum, who died at Auschwitz in November 1943 at the age of twenty-nine. Once she was yelled at by a young Gestapo officer. She wrote in her journal: 'I felt no indignation, rather a real compassion and would like to ask: "Did you have a very unhappy childhood, has your girlfriend let you down?"'* She was not fearful. She also had a deep sense of who the human person is. What makes a human person the sacred reality that the person is? Her deepest belief was that each person is a 'house' where God resides. At one moment she said, 'Everyone must be turned into a dwelling dedicated to you. I shall try to find a dwelling place and a refuge for you in as many houses as possible. There are so many empty houses. I shall prepare them all for You, the most honoured guest.'† She had a deep sense of the beauty of each person; she felt that each one was carrying the mystery of God in a capacity to be, to love and to be loved.

So what are we looking for? Are we prepared not only to love peace, but also to work for peace and to accept who we are in our fundamental poverty and our fundamental beauty?

---

*   Etty Hillesum, *An Interrupted Life: The Diaries, 1941-1943 and Letters*, New York: Henry Holt, 1996, p. 86.

†   Ibid., p. 213.

CHAPTER 4

Listening and Communication

Peace accords are beautiful things, but it is also important that people meet each other on a grassroots level. It's important to encourage people to come together to tell their stories, to say to them 'Tell me your story, your story of pain, your story of hope.'

I want to talk about a passage in the Gospel of Saint John that always moves me. John the Baptist sees Jesus and, looking at Jesus, says, 'Here is the Lamb of God who takes away the sin of the world.' I'd love to have seen Jesus then, his demeanour, how he walked. For the Jewish people the lamb has great significance. The blood of the lamb and the liberation of the Jewish people from slavery to walk towards the Promised Land. The slaughtered lamb. The lamb takes away sin.

Do you know what sin is? It's when there is a barrier between you and me. Between me and God, between me and myself. It is a wall, a wall so that we cannot speak to each other. We don't encounter others, because we are so certain that we are right; 'You have nothing to bring me. I don't need you.'

Then the next day John the Baptist sees Jesus again and says here is the Lamb of God who takes away this terrible barrier, which prevents us meeting ourselves, meeting the other, meeting truth and meeting God. At that moment two of the disciples break off from their master and teacher, John the Baptist. They start following Jesus. And the first words of Jesus in this Gospel, as he turns around are, 'What are you

looking for? What do you want?' (John 1:38)
These are the first words of Jesus to each of us.
'What do you want? What is it you want really?
What is deepest within you? Where is your
desire, your thirst, your hope?' Jesus doesn't tell
people what to do. He asks them a question.
'What are seeking as you begin to follow me?'

We have to begin to look at the places of
conflict, but that isn't easy. All of you know that
I am I, and you are you, and you've got your way
of doing things and I've got mine. Think how
quickly conflict can arise inside a family and
how people just shut off, living together without
any communication, frightened of communication, frightened of announcing, even
frightened of speaking to children! I was
accompanying a couple and they were telling me
about their daughter of seventeen who wanted
more money. I can imagine every seventeen-year-
old wants more money! I said to the parents,
'But have you put your cards on the table. Have
you said "This is how much we earn, this is how
much we have to pay for the car, this is what we
pay for this and that. There is not much money
left, so we can't give you much more"?' They
looked at me as if I was saying something
completely out of Mars or the moon! 'You don't

talk to children about money!' they said. But why not? That girl of seventeen is not stupid. Why can't we talk? Maybe you wouldn't talk to a five-year-old about finances, but why can't we put the cards on the table, why can't we be open, why can't there be dialogue?

I can understand that some young people in Ireland have a negative attitude towards their parents because they are angry and because there is no communication. I've never been a parent, but I see that it is difficult for parents to treat their child of twelve, not as if they are six years old, but as if they are twelve. The way a child communicates at twelve is different to the way a child communicates at six and at the age of seventeen. Communication is vital. Communication between husband and wife and communication between parents and children. We must listen to each other because that's where it all begins, the belief that the child is important. That's not to say, obviously, that we don't put down rules and regulations and all the rest, but it should be explained why we do it. The exercise of authority is to love, to help another to grow to freedom. Freedom comes as we move from fear to trust. That means that we have a listening heart.

Today everybody is stressed, everybody is running around, everybody is doing more and more. We are losing what I would call the 'sacred space of listening'. To be people of peace we have to be at peace in ourselves and to be at peace in ourselves is not just being quiet, it is finding that unity in ourselves between head and heart.

I was in Rwanda shortly after the genocide and the big question was, 'Where do we go from here?' It was obvious that the only answer would be for little groups of Tutsi and Hutu people, just a small group of six or seven people, to come together to say what they have lived and what they are hoping for. It is vital for Jews and Palestinians to talk together about what they have lived and are living, their pain, anger and depression. Let's talk about the pain of the war, the pain of losing a son or a father. Talk, because if we cannot talk, then the pain keeps boiling up within us. Whenever there are places of conflict, people must come together to share and to talk because we have to get out some of the things that we are living. We have to tell our story and we can only begin to talk when there is trust. Here in Northern Ireland the Corrymeela Community is bringing mothers together; the same thing is being done in Israel and Palestine between Palestinians and Jews. People are coming together to talk about how they have been hurt. Often when we have been hurt we either fall into depression or into violence. We close up in fury and sadness or we want revenge. But sometimes people decide, 'This can no longer continue. We must do something about it. We must learn to share and to build space.'

It is important to discover what it means to listen to others, to understand them, to understand how people function. It's not easy to see how another person functions. There is no point in just telling people what to do. We must discover how to enter into each other's story so that there is dialogue and mutual trust. That is a beginning. But it's still a long road and each of us has our own road on the journey to peace.

Let's try to understand each other. Tell me your story, the story of your pain, the story of your failures and I can tell you my story and somewhere we will be coming together. Forgiveness is a long road. It is based on the knowledge that each person is important, that each person is precious, that each person can change, that I can change and you can change. In the old days, we used to say, 'If you change I will love you.' Now we're beginning to say, 'If I love you, you will change and I too will change.' If you discover that somebody really loves you, really appreciates you, understands you, listens to you, then you begin to change. You come out from behind the barriers of fear you have constructed around your heart.

CHAPTER 5

Peace

We are in a world where we all want peace, and we all love peace. But the question will always be 'Are we prepared to work for it?' And to work for it can mean to put one's life in danger. It can mean to cross over barriers where one is not always understood or respected. Cross over the frontiers to meet the other, to encounter the other, to find the strength to listen to the other.

It is easy to want peace and love peace. It is easy to say, 'Leave me in peace', but are we prepared to struggle for peace, which would mean to enter into places of conflict in the family; in the community; wherever? And if we are prepared to enter into places of conflict, are we aware that we are vulnerable and can be hurt?

We can talk about peace, world peace, but we must also talk about peace in our families. We must talk about peace with our children. We must talk about peace as man helps woman to become fully herself and woman helps man to become fully himself, as parents love children so much that they help them to become fully themselves. Not just to enter a group, or a tribe, but to become fully human in communion with God, that's what God wants, for 'the glory of God is people fully alive'. The Word became flesh to bring us together. To bring us together in family, where we truly love each other. Not just the men going off to the pub to drink Guinness and the women left all alone; not just the men looking at television and football, but men and women together, loving each other and being a sign of God for each other. If our families are places of love; if parents and children are helping each other to become fully human, to become fully alive, then peace will come in our land. Peace will come between cultures; peace will come in our world.

We know what success is, but are we seeking success at the risk of damaging our humanity? I find that one of the most important things we are called to do as peacemakers is to find a style of living. How do we live? I see so many people in France who have to travel an hour and a half by car to work. They work and then they come home and they are absolutely pooped! When they come back home at perhaps eight o' clock at night they just put themselves in front of the television, because there is too much stress and too much fatigue. What does it mean to be stuck in front of the television and to receive images without any dialogue? We should try to find a style of life where we live peacefully, where we can find silence, because we cannot be at peace unless we cherish silence; silence in the family where we can be together and love each other.

In the prayer of Ecclesiastes there is time to be silent and time to talk, but talk must always come from the place of silence and not from a place of aggressiveness and power. It is quite obvious that when we are stressed, when we are fatigued, when we don't know how to eat well, when we don't know how to eat together and have fun, then we lose something of what it means to be a human being. If we want to be people of peace we have to know what it means to be a human being, to be mature, to love people, to contemplate, to love nature, to love children and to have fun with children. If parents are too busy working and never have time to go on their hands and knees and play with their children then they are losing something of their humanity.

There can be no peace unless we are all convinced that every person, whatever his or her abilities or disabilities, whatever his or her ethnic origins, culture or religion, is precious to God. In the heart of every human being there is a quest for truth, a quest for justice, a quest for peace, a quest for love, a quest for mercy. In the heart of each one of us we have this longing for something over and above our immediate reality. This longing for peace is very deep in the hearts of each one of us. We love truth. We want truth. We want justice. It is something that unites all human beings and can bring us together. This access to God, this possibility of being in relationship to God, links us all together. All things were made through God. The Word became flesh. The Word became a tiny child to break down those barriers, the dividing wall that prevents us shaking hands with those who are different. Behind those walls each group considers itself the best, the most important and the most loved by God. The Word became flesh to bring these barriers down so that all of us can discover that we are all precious to God and made for love.

God is forgiveness. God is mercy; we don't have to be frightened of God. God knows our brokenness, God knows how vulnerable we are, and God knows also the fear and violence that are within us. But he is inviting us to go deeper. I am always touched in the Gospel of John when after having appeared to Mary of Magdala, Jesus appears to the ten disciples and says to them 'peace to you, peace'. When Jesus says to us 'peace', it is a covenant relationship; Jesus *is* our peace. Jesus says to us, 'I'm with you. Don't worry. Whatever happens, I'll be with you. I'll look after you. All I ask of you is that you trust.' That reminds us of the text of Isaiah 43, 'Do not be afraid, for I have liberated you. I have called you by your name and you are mine. If you go through the waters, I'll be with you. If you go through the rivers, you won't be submerged. If you go through fire, you won't be burnt. If you go through the flame, you won't be consumed, for I am the Lord God of Israel, the Holy One, your redeemer and you are precious to my eyes and I love you.' So when Jesus says to his disciples and to us 'peace', he is saying, 'I am with you. I will always be with you. That is not to say that you won't suffer or have difficulties, that you won't be in conflict, but I will be with you. I'll give you the strength, I'll give you the love. So don't worry. I'll be with you.'

Then Jesus shows his disciples his wounds; I'm always touched by the realisation of the wounded body of Jesus because these wounds tell us something. They tell us about love. He went to the very end of love to be able to say to each one of us 'I love you'. But it is also telling us something about our own wounds, and our own difficulties in relationships. It will be through our wounds that God will give us his strength. Jesus doesn't want us to live in a cocoon. He sends us forth. He sends us out to be instruments of peace in the world of war. To be instruments of love in the world where there is so often hate or indifference. That doesn't mean sending us off to a far country, but sending us off in a new way in our family, in our school, place of work or parish. 'Then he breathes upon them and he says, "Receive the Spirit."' Receive a new power. We all need a new strength. We need this strength to help us to come out from behind the walls of fear so that we can open our hearts to the different, and meet the stranger.

Meeting the stranger does not mean just saying 'hello'; it is not just listening to his or her story. It is understanding them and to go even further: to appreciate the difference. Then we can enter into communion together. But there again it is a long road. So as the Father sent Jesus, Jesus sends us into a world where there is a lot of pain. Do you know what he sends us to do? To forgive. To become men and women of forgiveness. Forgiveness is not just saying, 'let's forget about it!', rather it's entering into a new relationship and understanding of where you are, listening to each other, getting closer to each other. Everyone feels guilty because they are not what they should be, or what they think they should be. Jesus came to relieve guilt and to help each of us discover that it is okay to be ourselves and then to grow, to become a man or woman of peace. To grow we need community. If we learn forgiveness we will then discover that it is a growth towards wholeness and holiness. Holiness is not hiding ourself and saying prayers. Holiness is becoming like Jesus and taking our place in the world to reveal that God is mercy; God is love, God has come to bring us together and wants us to be a people filled with hope, and also with joy. 'I say these things to you', says Jesus, 'so that your joy might be full and my joy might be within you.' (John 15)

CHAPTER 6

Celebrating Difference

Jesus called people together in love. He called people — irrespective of their religion or race — to eat at the same table and to enter into a relationship of friendship, which means letting down barriers.

Whatever our religion, or culture or abilities, one of the fundamental invitations of Jesus is 'Love your enemy. Do good to those who hate you.' What strikes me today is the number of humanitarian projects, which are in no way religious, where young people – and the less young – are going into situations of danger, or at least of difficulty, to help others and to engage with others. Jesus says 'Come and see'. The journey with Jesus is going to be a journey of transformation. We don't follow Jesus to be comfortable.

As we travel across the world we see how different people are. To a European, the Japanese seem very Japanese and the Chinese very Chinese. Perhaps we pop down into the Middle East, and find things again very different. If we travel down into Africa, we discover more difference. We go up through the Balkans, Kosovo and Serbia, and keep going and meet the French and the Italians. Then we go up into the British Isles and find Ireland and Northern Ireland. People are so different everywhere, and everyone thinks that their own culture is the best. So we build walls around ourselves, walls of language, of customs, and of how we relate to each other and how we relate to God.

If we're in a family in the Northern Hemisphere, normally we would tell children to eat with a knife and fork, am I right? Mummy or Daddy would say that it's not nice to eat with your hands! But then one day that little boy grows up and he goes to India and everybody there is eating with their hands! They find it crazy to eat with a bit of metal when they were given hands to eat with! Then he goes on a little further into China or Japan and they will be eating with little pieces of wood. Every culture is so different.

How can we move out from a belonging which closes us up and prevents us from opening up to others? I would like to share with you my own story of ecumenism, because I was brought up in a Catholic family without much contact with people who were Protestants or Anglicans. When I entered naval college as a young man, every morning when we were on parade they would say, 'Roman Catholics, fall out!' and we would take one step forward, turn right and say a 'Hail Mary', while everybody else was saying the 'Our Father'. Things have changed so much! I began L'Arche on very Catholic soil with a Dominican priest. Gradually we started meeting Protestant parents with handicapped children, and we began to open up. When we opened a community in Bethany (West Bank) near the mosque we started to work with Muslims and came in contact with Muslim parents. We started a community in Bangalore, and then later in Calcutta. In these communities live Hindus, Christians and Muslims. In Calcutta, we are based in a particular area, where on one side there are Muslims who are eating cows and on the other side are Hindus who are rearing pigs and if you know anything about this situation you know that it can be explosive! We are living right in the middle of this area: Christians, Hindus and Muslims living together as a sign of unity and peace. It is not always easy, but we are learning to make the journey.

Ecumenism is not just about everybody doing everything together. It's about Church of Ireland people loving their Church and knowing why they belong to that Church; Presbyterians loving their Church and knowing why they love their Church; Catholics loving their Church; the people of Northern Ireland loving Northern

Ireland and the beauty that is there. It means that we are all part of a culture and our flesh has been moulded by the culture, but at the same time we have to know why. I'm not just a Catholic because Mum and Dad are Catholics. It's important to love one's culture, to love one's faith and then to discover how that faith is calling us to open up, because our faith in God brings us to love every human person, whatever their abilities and disabilities, or whatever their religion.

At the heart of the message of Jesus is 'love your enemies, do good to those who hate you, speak well of those who speak evilly of you, pray for those who crush you and persecute you.' It sounds beautiful. Have you ever tried to say something nice about somebody you know is criticising you behind your back? Try to say something nice about that person. You'll find your glands will swell up and you won't be able to do it because if we are being attacked we must protect ourselves. So we create these barriers and we can only begin to open up and love the enemy if somebody else defends us. You know one of the translations of the word 'paraclete' is 'defender', 'the one who defends'? We don't have to protect ourselves if we know that God is protecting us.

CHAPTER 7

Reconciliation and Change

*Jesus is our peace and he came to bring us
together. He came to touch our hearts, to lead
us into a reality over and above our own
group, our own culture, to bring us into a
friendship with God. He came to lead us to the
God who created us — who created flowers,
insects, mountains, elephants, the whole
universe — and who loves each one of us. Jesus
came to introduce us to truth, justice, mercy,
forgiveness and love.*

I have had the privilege, through 'L'Arche' and 'Faith and Light', to visit many different cultures. While I was in Rwanda shortly after the genocide a young woman came up to me and told me that seventy-five members of her family had been assassinated. She said, 'I have so much anger and hate within me and I don't know what to do with it. Everybody is talking about reconciliation, but nobody has asked any forgiveness. I just don't know what to do with all the hate that is within me.' I said, 'I understand. I understand.' What more can one say to a young woman like that who suddenly finds herself all alone because all her family has been killed? The problem for her was that she felt guilty because she didn't know how to forgive and so she was caught up in the world of hate and depression. I said to her, 'Do you know that the first step towards forgiveness is "no vengeance"? Do you want to kill those who killed members of your family?' 'No,' she answered, 'There is too much death.' I said, 'Well, that is the first step in the process of forgiveness. The first step.'

Forgiveness is a journey, it is not just an event. The first step in peace-making is 'no vengeance'. Then gradually it is to enter into a relationship with those who have hurt us. We say in the 'Our Father': forgive us as we forgive others. Forgive us for we too have hurt others and we have hurt God. Forgive us.

There is a story in the Gospel that I consider extremely moving. During his last meal with the disciples Jesus got up and took off his outer garments, went to fetch a basin. He put water in the basin, knelt down in front of the disciples and washed their feet. Jesus was revealing that God comes and kneels before us. What does that mean? When we live through tragic events we can say, 'Where is God? Why doesn't God do something about this?' People on both sides of dividing lines pray. In Northern Ireland, both Catholics and Protestants pray. Why this silence of God? This has brought some people to think that maybe there is no God, because God is so silent. We sometimes talk about the silence of God in the face of the tragedies of this world, the tragic deaths, and the killings. Where is God and what is he doing? God is kneeling at our feet and saying, 'I will give you strength so that you may bring peace.' I believe that this mystery of Jesus kneeling at our feet is about humility. It's about peace-making. Maybe we become peacemakers when we are no longer struggling for power, to be at the top, but just working to serve each other. Maybe we cannot all stand in situations of warfare and be men and women of non-violence in painful situations. Maybe we cannot all do big things, but all of us can kneel at each other's feet and say, 'I trust you and I believe you.' All of us can ask the spirit of God to come within us, to give us the strength, the wisdom, the humility, to help people to rise up and to believe in themselves. The danger for all of us is that we are living in a culture of competition and rivalry, so we are often on the defensive and trying to prove that we are better than others are. Have we forgotten that Jesus is kneeling at our feet asking us to serve each other just where we are?

I think I can understand Peter who looked at Jesus and said, 'You, wash my feet?' Jesus replied, 'You cannot understand now, but you'll know later.' Then Peter said, 'No. You shall never wash my feet.' It's because he can't really understand Jesus. He can't understand that Jesus came to bring a totally new order where the walls would fall down and we would come together as brothers and sisters. Do we understand this new order? Do we understand God's vision for humanity or are we just closed up in our own little worlds? Can peace come? Is there hope for Kosovo, Israel, Palestine, Iraq or Northern Ireland? Is there hope in this world where the gap between the rich and the poor is growing daily? Is there hope? Yes, there is hope! There is hope because God is. God is! And though there is the silence of God, there is also the mystery of God working in the hearts of people doing beautiful things. They don't hit the headlines. The headlines are frequently things of pain — catastrophies, death. We don't see all the peace-loving people breaking down the barriers to work together and to love each other. All of us can understand the reaction of Peter. Maybe if we found Jesus kneeling at our feet we would react in the same way. We want a big God who fixes our problems. We don't want a little God saying, 'I need you and I'll come and live in you. I'll give you a new strength, a new spirit and you shall work so people become free and loving and peace-making.' We always want a God who is going to fix our problems, but God is saying, 'I'll give you the strength so you become one of those who work with others to bring peace to our world.'

There are many hungry people in our world. God is not going to send down some bread from the trees, because if somebody is hungry, it's our problem. If somebody is sick, it's my problem; it's your problem. If somebody is closed up in an institution because he has a disability it's *my* problem; it's *your* problem; it's *our* problem. We have to do something about it. If people have a toothache, you don't just pray for him or her, you take them to a good dentist. And Jesus says to us: 'It's up to you to do something about it, but I will give you my spirit. I'll give you a new force, a new strength, and a new wisdom so that you can break down the dividing walls of hostility.' It's up to you and me, but God will give us strength if we open our hearts to him and ask for that strength. We hear about the presence of God in the stories that are told of people struggling to bring peace. God trusts us so much and loves us so much; he wants us to become men and women who can receive forgiveness and give forgiveness, who can receive wisdom and give wisdom. Jesus kneeling before his disciples is a revelation of Jesus kneeling at our feet saying, 'I trust you, I believe in you, I love you' and calling us to stand up and to work for love.

The frontiers that separate people from each other can come down if we open our hearts to this vulnerable God. Jesus sent us the Spirit, to change our hearts of stone into hearts of flesh. He became weak and was crucified and died on the cross. The message of Jesus is transformation. He calls us to open up to others. So the big question will always be, 'Do we want to change? Do we want to open our hearts to the different?'